# WORLD MYTHOLOGY

# HERCULES

Adele D. Richardson

**Consultant:**
Dr. Laurel Bowman
Department of Greek and Roman Studies
University of Victoria, British Columbia

Capstone
press

Mankato, Minnesota

Capstone Press
151 Good Counsel Drive, P.O. Box 669, Mankato, Minnesota 56002
http://www.capstone-press.com

*Library of Congress Cataloging-in-Publication Data*
Richardson, Adele, 1966–
    Hercules / Adele D. Richardson.
      p. cm.—(World mythology)
    Summary: Relates the exploits of Hercules and his importance in Roman mythology,
including his connection to such figures as King Augeas and Queen Hippolyte, and
describes the role of myths in the modern world.
Includes bibliographical references and index.
      ISBN 0-7368-1611-9 (hardcover)
      1. Hercules (Roman mythology)—Juvenile literature. [1. Hercules (Roman mythology)
2. Mythology, Roman.] I. Title. II. Series.
BL820.H5 R52 2003
292.2'113—dc21                                                          2002008464

**Editorial Credits**
Blake A. Hoena, editor; Karen Risch, product planning editor; Juliette Peters, designer and
      illustrator; Alta Schaffer, photo researcher

**Photo Credits**
Art Resource/Réunion des Musées Nationaux, 16
Bridgeman Art Library/British Museum, London, 14; Musee des Beaux-Arts, Nantes,
      France, 18; Prado, Madrid, Spain, 20
Corbis/Araldo de Luca, cover, 4, 6; Ruggero Vanni, 8; Art & Immagini srl, 12

1 2 3 4 5 6 08 07 06 05 04 03

# TABLE OF CONTENTS

4

Statues often
show Hercules
holding a
wooden club.
He used
this weapon
in battles.

Hercules (HUR-kyoo-leez) was a famous hero in Roman myths. Stories about Hercules also were popular in ancient Greece. The Greeks called him Heracles (HER-uh-kleez). Today, his Roman name is more common.

Ancient Greeks and Romans considered Hercules the strongest man who ever lived. Hercules often used his great strength to help people. He protected people from mythical monsters and other dangers. In myths, he helped make the world safe for people.

Ancient Greeks and Romans believed in many gods. They believed the gods controlled everything that happened in the world. The most powerful gods were the Olympians. These 12 gods ruled the world from Mount Olympus. This mountain is in Greece.

People often prayed to the gods for help. Hercules became a god after his death. People asked him for good luck on their quests.

This statue was created around A.D. 195. It shows Hercules as a child. He is choking the snakes Hera sent to kill him.

# THE BIRTH OF HERCULES

Hercules' father was Zeus (ZOOSS). Zeus was ruler of the Olympians and married to Hera (HER-uh). Hera was the goddess of marriage and childbirth.

Zeus was not a loyal husband to Hera. He fell in love with Alcmene (alk-ME-nee). This woman was from Thebes, Greece. She was Hercules' mother.

Hera hated the children Zeus had with other goddesses or women. She often tried to punish these children. Hera especially disliked Hercules. She hated Hercules because he was one of Zeus' most powerful children.

When Hercules was a baby, Hera sent two snakes to kill him. Hercules woke as the snakes crawled into his crib. He grabbed the snakes around their necks and choked them. He was given the name Hercules after killing the snakes. Hercules means "glory of Hera."

Delphi was an ancient Greek city. Apollo had a temple in Delphi. Apollo was the Greek and Roman god of youth and music. He was the god who spoke through the Oracle of Delphi.

# THE ORACLE'S COMMAND

Zeus often talked about Hercules' great strength. His bragging angered Hera. She hated Hercules so much that one day she made him go crazy. Hera wanted to show everyone that Hercules was not as great as Zeus said he was.

In his madness, Hercules thought everyone was his enemy. By mistake, he killed his wife and sons. Hercules was filled with guilt when he realized what he had done.

Hercules then went to the Oracle of Delphi (DEL-fye). In myths, gods spoke to people through oracles. The gods used these temples to tell people how to solve their problems.

Hercules asked the Oracle of Delphi how he could be forgiven for killing his family. The oracle told Hercules to go live with his cousin, King Eurystheus (yoo-RISS-thee-uhss). Hercules had to do whatever the king asked him to do.

Eurystheus was jealous of Hercules' fame. He gave Hercules 12 tasks that he thought were impossible to perform. These tasks became known as Hercules' 12 labors.

# GREEK and ROMAN *Mythical Figures*

Greek Name: **APOLLO**
Roman Name: **APOLLO**
God of youth and music

Greek Name: **ATLAS**
Roman Name: **ATLAS**
Titan who holds the heavens above
the earth

Greek Name: **HERA**
Roman Name: **JUNO**
Zeus' wife and goddess of marriage
and childbirth

Greek Name: **HERACLES**
Roman Name: **HERCULES**
Greek hero famous for performing
his 12 labors

Greek Name: **ODYSSEUS**
Roman Name: **ULYSSES**
Greek hero whose adventures are
told of in Homer's *The Odyssey*

Greek Name: **ZEUS**
Roman Name: **JUPITER**
Hercules' father and ruler of
the Olympians

# QUEST MYTHS

Ancient Greeks and Romans told several types of myths. Explanation myths told why events like earthquakes and storms happened. Creation myths told how the world, gods, and people were created.

Stories about heroes are known as quest myths. In these myths, heroes completed nearly impossible tasks. Quest myths were told to encourage people to work hard. Quest myths taught people that they should never give up even if a task seemed impossible.

Many famous quest myths exist. The Greek poet Homer told of important quest myths in his long poems *The Iliad* and *The Odyssey*. *The Iliad* tells about the last year of the Trojan War. The Greeks attacked the city of Troy during this war. *The Odyssey* tells of Odysseus' (oh-DISS-ee-uhss) journey home after the Trojan War. Hercules' 12 labors are also famous quest myths.

Hercules killed the Nemean Lion for his first labor. In art, Hercules sometimes is shown wearing a cape made of a lion's skin. He wore the lion's head as a helmet. Some myths say the cape and helmet came from the Nemean Lion.

For the first labor, King Eurystheus told Hercules to kill the Nemean (NEE-mee-uhn) Lion. The lion's skin was very tough. Weapons could not harm the lion. Hercules had to wrestle the lion with his bare hands to kill it.

Hercules had to kill the many-headed hydra (HYE-druh) for his second task. Each time Hercules cut off one of this monster's heads, two more heads grew back. Hercules asked his nephew Iolaus (eye-oh-LAY-uhss) to help him kill the hydra. Hercules would cut off one of the hydra's heads. Iolaus then burned the wound with fire. The fire stopped more heads from growing back.

For his next labors, Hercules had to capture two mythical animals. Hercules chased the Arcadian (ar-CAY-dee-uhn) Stag for a year before he captured it. This white deer had golden horns. Hercules captured the Erymanthian (er-i-MAN-thee-uhn) Boar by chasing it into a snowbank. He then trapped this large, wild pig with a net.

Myths say King Diomedes' horses attacked and ate people. In this statue, Hercules is taming the king's horses.

# THE NEXT FOUR LABORS

Hercules cleaned King Augeas' (aw-JEE-uhss) stables for his fifth labor. The stables had not been cleaned in 30 years, and more than 3,000 oxen lived in them. King Eurystheus gave Hercules one day to complete this task. Hercules forced two rivers to flow through the stables. The water quickly swept away the mess.

For his sixth labor, Hercules killed the Stymphalian (stim-FAY-lee-uhn) Birds. These birds had metal feathers and ate people. Hercules shot them out of the air with his bow and arrows.

Hercules captured animals for his next two tasks. One animal was a huge bull that lived on the island of Crete. Hercules then captured the horses of King Diomedes (dye-uh-ME-deez). The king was very cruel to his horses. The horses became mean and attacked people. Hercules threw the cruel king to his horses. They quickly attacked and killed the king. Once the king was dead, the horses became tame.

Artists often show scenes from myths in their art. This vase shows Hercules taking Cerberus to King Eurystheus. The king was afraid of Cerberus and hid in a giant vase.

# THE LAST FOUR LABORS

Hercules' last four labors began by stealing the golden belt from the Amazon Queen Hippolyte (hi-PAWL-i-tuh). The Amazons were a group of female warriors.

Hercules captured Geryon's (GER-ee-uhn) cattle for his tenth labor. Geryon was a monster with three heads and three bodies. Hercules killed Geryon and took the cattle.

Next, Hercules had to get the golden apples grown by the Hesperides (hess-PER-i-deez). These nymphs were daughters of Atlas (AT-lass), the Titan who held the heavens on his shoulders. No one but Atlas knew where his daughters lived. Hercules asked him for help. Hercules offered to hold the heavens while Atlas went to get the apples from his daughters.

Lastly, Hercules captured Cerberus (SUR-bur-uhss). This three-headed dog guarded the Underworld. After finishing his last task, the gods forgave Hercules for killing his wife and sons.

In the painting *Death of Nessus*, Jules Elie Delaunay shows Hercules killing the centaur Nessus. Centaurs were mythical creatures with the body and legs of a horse. They had the upper body of a man.

Hercules went to Thebes after he finished his labors. There, he married a woman named Deianira.

One day, Hercules and Deianira were traveling together. The centaur Nessus (NESS-uhss) came along and tried to kidnap Deianira. Hercules shot Nessus with a bow and arrow.

Before Nessus died, he told Deianira that his blood was magical. She could use it to make a love charm. This charm would make Hercules love her always.

Deianira worried that Hercules might stop loving her. She made the love charm. She then sprinkled it on Hercules' clothes. When Hercules put the clothes on, his skin began to burn. Nessus had lied. The blood actually was poison.

Zeus saw what had happened. He did not want his son to suffer. He sent down a cloud to bring Hercules to Mount Olympus. There, Zeus made his son immortal and Hercules became a god.

People often create art to represent exciting stories in myth. Francisco de Zurbaran's painting shows Hercules (center) fighting the hydra. Iolaus is holding a torch to burn the hydra's wounds after Hercules cuts off its heads.

# MYTHOLOGY TODAY

Myths still influence the world today. The planets in our solar system are named after Roman gods. Jupiter is Zeus' Roman name. It also is the name of the solar system's largest planet. Many groupings of stars are named after mythical characters. Hercules is the name of one constellation.

Things in nature also share the names of mythical characters. The Hercules beetle lives in North and South America. It can grow up to 8 inches (20 centimeters) long.

Mentions of Hercules are found in the words people use. A "herculean" task is a job that seems impossible to do. A person who works very hard on a task is said to make a "herculean" effort.

Stories about Hercules and his adventures are popular today. Books have been written about his 12 labors. TV shows and movies retell his adventures. People often enjoy listening to stories about Hercules and other mythical heroes.

Adriatic Sea

•Rome

**ITALY**

N
W • E
S

**GREECE**

•Troy

Aegean Sea

ITHACA

Thebes
•

Athens

Ionian Sea

Sparta
•

DELOS

**KEY**

• City

🏛 Oracle of Delphi

⛰ Mount Olympus

▨ Region of Attica

CRETE

Mediterranean Sea

SCALE
Miles
0        100        200

0    100    200
Kilometers

# WORDS TO KNOW

**ancient** (AYN-shunt)—very old

**boar** (BOR)—a wild pig

**centaur** (SEN-tor)—a creature that is half man and half horse

**charm** (CHARM)—an object people believe will bring good luck

**constellation** (kon-stuh-LAY-shuhn)—a group of stars that forms a shape

**immortal** (i-MOR-tuhl)—able to live forever

**kidnap** (KID-nap)—to take and keep a person against his or her will

**oracle** (OR-uh-kuhl)—a place that a god speaks through; in myths, gods used oracles to tell people how to solve problems.

**quest** (KWEST)—a journey taken by a hero to perform a task

**stag** (STAG)—an adult male deer

**Titan** (TYE-ten)—one of the giants who ruled the world before the Olympians

**Underworld** (UHN-dur-wurld)—the place under the ground where the souls of the dead went

# READ MORE

**Burleigh, Robert.** *Hercules.* San Diego: Silver Whistle, 1999.

**Hoena, B. A.** *Zeus.* World Mythology. Mankato, Minn.: Capstone Press, 2003.

# USEFUL ADDRESSES

**National Junior Classical League**
Miami University
Oxford, OH  45056

**Ontario Classical Association**
2072 Madden Boulevard
Oakville, ON  L6H 3L6
Canada

# INTERNET SITES

Track down many sites about Hercules.
Visit the FACT HOUND at *http://www.facthound.com*

**IT IS EASY!   IT IS FUN!**

1) Go to *http://www.facthound.com*
2) Type in: 0736816119
3) Click on "FETCH IT" and FACT HOUND
   will find several links hand-picked by our editors.

**Relax and let our pal FACT HOUND do the research for you!**

# INDEX